Dear Rockstar,

52 INSPIRATIONAL LETTERS AND DESIGNS TO ROCK YOUR LIFE!

Written By
PAM HOELZLE

Illustrated By
ALICIA FEINBERG

Cover by Alicia Feinberg

DEDICATIONS

Pam dedicates this book to Rosie & Zach

You are my miracles. May you always believe, hope
and have the courage to dream BIG.

Alicia dedicates this book to Mike & Ryder

Mike, for being on my team, always and forever.
Ryder, may you always dream big, work hard, and be kind.

Introduction

As I watched my 24-year old daughter bend her way into marichyasana c while she prepared to teach in the 200-hour yoga teacher training she and I were attending in Bali, my eyes welled, glassy.

What a blessing to be in Asia, to be immersed in this practice, two teachers now learning together; the young one and her determined Mother.

If only, my mind whispered as the tears raced down my cheeks.
If only my mother and I had an opportunity like this...
if only we could have... traveled before.

I was now older than my mother had been when she died.
I couldn't remember a week in the past twenty-five years since her passing when I hadn't wanted to hear her voice, sit across the table from her and laugh, laugh with her.

If only she had left me some instructions, letters even.

As my daughter's dark, curly brown hair bounced into the bathroom, I exhaled.

Someday, it would be me, saying goodbye to her and my other Rockstar child. Someday, further down the road, they'd be saying goodbye to their own children.

Wiping my face, I decided. I'd write the letters...
I'd write the letters my mom never had the time to write.
I'd share what I'd learned. I would.

YOU ARE A
Rockstar

RESUSCITATE
EACHOTHER

LOVE RIOT

JOB
SECURITY
IS A *LIE*

PASSION   PURPOSE

CONTRIBUTION   THE BEST IN

GUILT

INHABIT YOUR
Breath

"I don't know what
I don't know."

COMMUNITY

TRANSFORM
UPLIFT
INSPIRE
WRITE
TEACH
encourage
ReStore

CHOOSE
JOY

LIFE CEO

TRUST
HOLDS US
TOGETHER

learning
FAIL·URE
noun
1. the acquisition of knowledge
and/or skills through experiences,
which can be painful.

Gratitude
Junkie

YOU ARE A

Rockstar

Dear Rockstar,

It didn't take long.

Once you heard the music, you knew what you would be.
You'd be a Rockstar.
Born to rock, you were.
And, of course, you were right, dear.

And then, life zigged when you expected it to zag,
and instead of auditioning for The Voice, you were left stocking shelves.

In a sea of eight billion, it's easy to feel small, even insignificant
especially when you're left at the register while others earn the applause.

Perhaps you aren't a Rockstar in the tabloid kind of way.
Perhaps your bank account sucks and your achievements are lacking.

But Dear, don't fear.
Your Rockstar status is independent of results and other people's opinions.

BORN TO ROCK, YES, YOU WERE.
BORN TO SHARE THE MUSIC INSIDE.

All of life is your stage, Dear.
Your talents, experiences, and skills are your instruments.

Born to rock your one precious life, like no one prior,
like no one after... ever will.

DEAR ROCKSTAR,

A man held in a police chokehold cries, "I can't breathe."
A grown man cries for his mama as a knee ends his life.
A young girl advertises herself and is trafficked across state lines.
A virus spreads.

Oh Dear, sometimes good goes missing and bad goes on such a tear
you can't imagine any of us worthy of redemption.

In times like this, you must stand.
Yes, stand, Dear.
Refuse to look away. Acknowledge wrong, injustice and
empathize with those who are oppressed.
Name it. Make it your business.

You, me, the girl who lied to you and that guy who votes differently,
each of us is responsible for what takes place in our homes, at work in our
cities and nations.

This is the time to come together, to be the beloved community.

> **"The end is reconciliation; the end is redemption;
> the end is the creation of the Beloved Community.
> It is this type of spirit and this type of love that
> can transform opponents into friends. It is this
> type of understanding, goodwill that will transform
> the deep gloom of the old age into the exuberant
> gladness of the new age. It is this love which will
> bring about miracles in the hearts of men."**
>
> Martin Luther King

What is life, if all around people, people can't breathe?

Now, now is the time to resuscitate each other, Dear.

DEAR ROCKSTAR,

From the moment you took your very first step, I prayed that you would be led.
That wisdom would lead you, and love, love would find you.

As you moved beyond my care, I worried about your safety.
And the Divine, the Divine assured me, you'd be fine.

Then you left for a distant land and I was reminded,
you were never my possession and I, I was never your creator.

You my dear, arrived on this planet as Love's child
and that, that's how you'll leave it.

As a human, you've been invited to the greatest experiment of all.
Inside of every project, relationship, and circumstance,
lurks a higher purpose invisible to the naked eye, an invitation to LOVE.

All of life masquerades as an opportunity for LOVE's children.

So go ahead,
wherever you go,
whatever you do,

ignite a LOVE RIOT, dear.

JOB SECURITY IS A LIE

DEAR ROCKSTAR,

For as long as I can remember, I was going to be the first in my family to get a degree so I could get a job, and a job would save me...NOT.

And since statistics don't lie, did you know this generation is saddled with 1.5 trillion dollars of education debt? Sixty-four percent of us have either multiple jobs or non-traditional ones. And IBM employed 53,000 employees to achieve a billion dollar valuation, whereas Facebook achieved this with only 13,000 employees.

This is not your grandfather's economy, Dear.

Technology, global connectivity, and the virus have changed work forever. No degree, employer, or government program will save you.

Instead, you must shift.

Shift your mindset.
Shift to taking responsibility for creating your benefits and income streams.
Shift from consuming to creating
From a job taker to a job creator.
From an employee to a BOSS.

Shift to ownership.

Because job security, job security, is a lie, Dear.

DEAR ROCKSTAR,

I believe we are spirit.

I believe in the One.

In the WILL that is greater than me.

Matter of fact, I credit it for bringing us together.

And because you are every bit as free as I am, free to believe as
you choose. I encourage you to read these letters and take what inspires you
and leave what doesn't.

My hope is by making apparent, what wasn't to me, I can help
even accelerate you on your journey to making, making a life you love.

SUCCESS

MUTE THE
NAYSAYERS

BE
UNAPOLOGETIC

LIVE
AUTHENTICALLY

ON YOUR TERMS

Dear Rockstar,

All around you, the world shouts, do something, get rich, cure cancer, get elected, be on the cover of Sports Illustrated or Time, or marry someone that has.

I used to define success as winning, and then I won and didn't stay true to myself.

Dear, refuse to allow the media's definition of success; wealth, beauty, and power to influence yours.

Can you imagine having all the riches the world has to offer and losing your health? And what if you were on the cover of every fashion magazine but hated yourself?

Mute the voices shouting for you to be this, or have that.
Instead, listen to the still, small whisper within.
To thyself and thy Creator be true.

BE UNAPOLOGETIC.

Define success on your terms, Dear.

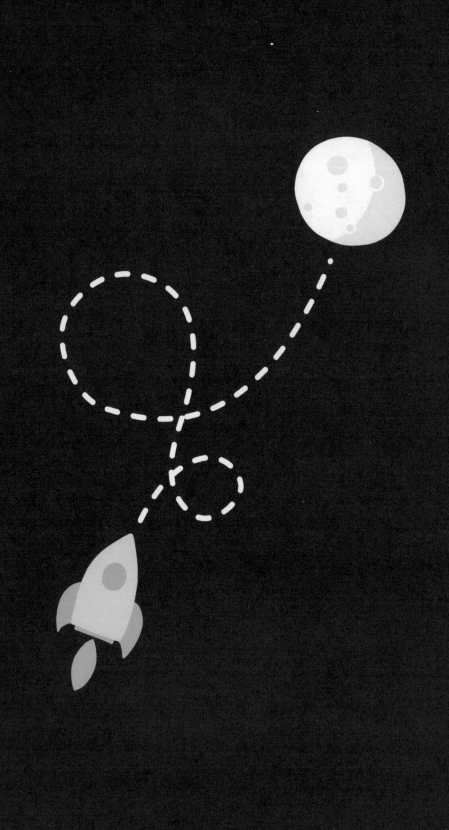

Dear Rockstar,

I wish when I arrived on the planet, the Divine had stamped "Permanent Beta" on my forehead. Maybe then I would have understood the goal in life isn't to be perfect, have all the right answers, or even have it all together.

As you work to leave your mark on the world, I hope you'll remember this lesson, this lesson that's taken me so long to learn.

Your grandma's apple pie, the one with chocolate chips, now that, my Dear, gets baked. And that poetry chapbook you're writing, it will be finished, even perfected.

But you, you will never be "done."

So, go ahead, give yourself permission to be unfinished, not quite all the way cooked, messy even.

Live each moment as an invitation to grow into the person, you always imagined yourself becoming.

What happens in the process makes the result all the sweeter, savor every second of this becoming, Dear.

Dear Rockstar,

I remember the time I was called to the Christian school you were attending, and within 20 minutes, you and I were standing on the curb. Kicked out, you, I mean, we were.

To add insult to injury, the administrators, the one's I'd been paying to introduce you to God, forbid you from ever coming on the property again.

As I stared into your shell-shocked, shamed, not entirely innocent eyes, I reminded you that regardless of what they did, you were free to choose how to respond.

For most of my life, I jumped from stimulus to reaction from situation to response, compulsively. I was a victim of circumstances until the day I chose otherwise.

This was the day, the day I moved from being everyone's puppet to freedom. Nothing, not spiritual hypocrites, nor prison, torture, disease, discrimination, or injustice of any kind can rob you of your fundamental freedom, Dear.

You are never forced to react.
You are never forced to repay evil with evil.
You are never forced to believe what others say about you or others.

Much of life lies outside of your control.

And still, you are always free, free to choose your response and who you will be in this moment, Dear.

Dear Rockstar,

When you were little, there were things that called to you,
music, frilly dresses, books, and *Beauty and The Beast*.
There were other things that repelled you,
snakes, loud people, and dinner without dessert.

You Dear, are unique, one in well, billions.

There will be things that grab your heart and pierce your soul; there will be.
And other things you'll barely notice, or if you do, you'll hardly care.

There will be tears only you can dry
people only you can love,
problems only you can solve
art only you can create,
opportunities only you can seize,
teams only you can join.

Life will be your teacher; your job is to pay attention,
to what calls to you and makes your heart sing.

This, this is how you make a life... a life you love, Dear.

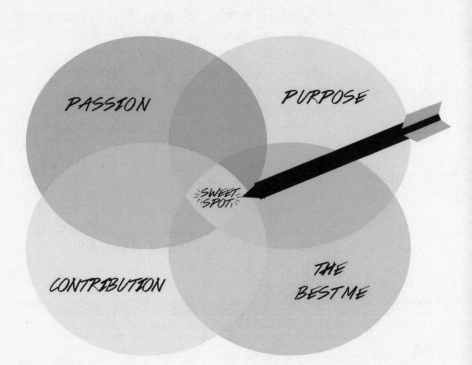

Dear Rockstar,

A while back, I started over, after already having lived four decades.

And everyone had an opinion as to what I should do and should not do.
Voices all around shouted for me to play it safe, do what I'd already done,
to be practical, realistic...even.
I listened and promptly muted everyone.

Once it quieted down, I tuned into the voice whispering inside of me.
Disappointed by life, I was desperate to wriggle free from the person I'd
been and to discover a truer truth. Mary Oliver's question led me.

"What is it you plan to do with your one wild and precious life?"

I drafted lists.
I marked things off which no longer made sense.
Like an onion, I peeled back the layers and allowed what had been to
slough off.
I wanted to pick up my kids at 2 pm, didn't want a nanny raising my kids,
didn't want to take a job where I had to travel out of town. And I wanted
to help other people create authentic lives similar to what I craved. The
process helped me find my sweet spot. Whenever you find yourself stuck,
at an intersection, or losing motivation, reflect on your sweet spot, Dear.

PASSION

What are you passionate about?

Not those things you are merely content with but rather those that make you lose track of time?

What are the things you'd do for free?

PURPOSE

Imagine the bigger picture, the bigger game, the reason, your WHY, why you were born.

What matters, what is meaningful and fulfilling, Dear?

CONTRIBUTION

Now imagine all the needs and wants, problems and challenges in the world.

What can you solve, how can you serve, add value to others and create revenues for yourself and your family?

THE BEST ME

When you do them, what things allow you to show up the very best version of yourself?

What, when you do it reflects you, the you, you most want to be?

SWEET SPOT

The place where you come fully alive, the place where
you can invest yourself and create a life of meaning,
contribution, an authentic life that maximizes your
life return on investment and allows you to grow into
the person you always imagined yourself becoming.

DEAR ROCKSTAR,

There was your first step, your first word, your first cookie,
that first story, and before I knew it... you were a poet.
You had me at goo-goo, and well, by the time you wrote your first
rhyme, I was convinced... you, you were divine.

How can you possibly be sure, you wonder.

It's simple. In the time before you, there was me without you, and
then there was you. And well, I can tell you with all certainty,
your birth was a miracle, Dear.

You want more evidence, do you?

What if I told you that you are one in eight billion. And based on
probability theory, you're even more extraordinary? The experts say the
chance of you being you, and all your ancestors being exactly who they
are, is one in four trillion.

One in four trillion, Rockstar, that's the probability of you being you, with
your parents who they are and your great, great, great grandparents
who they were.

So you see, either way, one in eight billion or one in four trillion, it's clear
you aren't some colossal mistake or even average.

You, my Dear, are a miracle.
Precious.
Valuable.
And irreplaceable.

When life blows in evidence that differs, remind yourself there was a time
before you, and there will be a time after you. And then seize the miracle
of your one in four trillion life.

GUILT

DEAR ROCKSTAR,

When you colored outside the lines, I applauded.
When you disagreed, I listened.
When you fell, I cleaned your wounds.

Grace.
Unmerited and undeserved she is, and well she is.
One day when I was face down in a bed of regret, Grace whisked in, in her supersized, life whiteout, kind of way.

She offered me a choice. I could continue to suffer under the slave masters of merit, performance, and achievement. I could continue to climb ladders in hopes of love, acceptance, even redemption. Or I, I could accept her and what she had to offer.

And that's when Grace pulled out her supply of life whiteout.
She explained that with her, I'd never run out of favor.
All the uglies, the ugly things I'd done, could be blotted out.

Shaking my head, I listened for the catch.
But instead of a one-two punch, Grace went to work rewinding through my past. As she sped through the errors, mistakes, and the hurts of yesterday, I watched guilt disappear. And then, with a flip of her wrist, she fast-forwarded into my future, into the mistakes I was yet to make.
She blotted out everything.

And then Grace turned to me and handed me that supersized bottle of life whiteout, she did. And before she let go of that bottle, she made me promise to accept what I could not yet understand. And to marinate, get all comfortable with her unconditional nature. And then, with a wink, she admitted, there was a catch... I knew it.

Now, what I'd received. I was to give away.
Try I was, to out give....the giver of all.
Grace.

INHABIT YOUR

Breath

DEAR ROCKSTAR,

I swear, I wish I knew how to breathe, to really inhabit my breath,
back, before you were born. But I didn't.
Back then, I ricocheted between holding my breath and hyperventilating.

It took decades of living as if life were a race before I found
myself in Bali, training to be a yoga instructor. It was here, here
on the coast, after hundreds of hours of yoga practice,
that I found myself arriving, as if for the first time in my breath.

Bending, twisting, wriggling, and maneuvering, at rest, sleep, and
play, life transformed from something I did to something I was.

Dear, did you know you can be deeply unconscious, a fit of
activity, a body running here and there, and not experiencing any of it?
You can be connected, connected to all those devices, and
disconnected from all, all that matters.

But there is another way. Why not practice?
Close your mouth and inhale through your nose, counting to five as you
watch your chest rise and your lungs fill. And now with your mouth closed,
exhale, press your diaphragm to your back, and match the length of your
exhale to your inhale. Now, do it again. And again. And now again gentler.

Watch your thoughts as they come and go, refusing to attach to them.
Now this time, as you inhale, ask the Divine to fill you with more of what
you desire; love, forgiveness, compassion, honesty, wisdom, patience, or
something specific.

As your lungs and chest fill, receive what you've requested.
And on your next exhale, let go, rid yourself of what no longer serves.

Inhabit your breath, Dear.

learning ~~FAIL·URE~~

noun

1. the acquisition of knowledge and/or skills through experiences, which can be painful.

Dear Rockstar,

I was once expected to win state but instead didn't get out of the semi-finals.
Back home after the race, I hid, afraid to show my face.
I'd failed and done it, oh so publicly.
Humiliated, I was pretty sure that losing, losing would be the death of me.

Fast forward a couple of decades when my 16-year marriage ended, my
business closed, and both of my Rockstar children rebelled.

LIFE IS MOSTLY NOT WHAT YOU THOUGHT...
NOT WHAT YOU ORDERED, DEAR.

The good news is, failure doesn't kill you even though it feels as if it may.
Sure, it will bruise your ego and smash your rose-colored glasses. But it also
helps develop the single most important muscle group in all of life, your 'get
back up' muscles. And these muscles transform failure into learning, Dear.

As long as you rise every time you fall, as long as you refuse to stay down...
there is no failure.

And this is why I don't believe in the "F" word.
There is no failure, only learning, Dear.

PERFECTLY
IMPERFECT

DEAR ROCKSTAR,

The other day, I overheard you beating yourself up and whipping yourself into a frenzy. Listening took me back, back to a time when I too expected perfection.

I was an anxious youngster who developed the unfortunate habit of pulling her hair out. Middle school is hard enough; imagine it with bald patches. My bald patches screamed, *something is wrong.*
And I knew, I knew what I had to do.
I would fix it. I would. I'd prove I was normal, good enough...even perfect.

And well those beliefs created an addict. They did.
I became addicted to work, running, health, learning, self-improvement, and heck, if it claimed to make life better I became obsessed. I did.

I was the hamster, perfectionism the hamster wheel. Sicker and sicker I got until the day, entirely burnt out, I chose to replace more and faster with less. I chose to make time for the quiet and chose praying, meditating, practicing yoga, long walks, and plenty of time in nature.

Soon, there I was, bald patches and all not afraid of who I was, capable of kindness and understanding for my exhausted, addicted self.

Perfection is a lie.

You are perfectly imperfect, Dear.

WHAT IF?

Dear Rockstar,

I have no idea why we refuse to talk about dying till we, or someone we love, does. Maybe, we think talking about it will speed its arrival. Or maybe we're just scared, scared to death of expiring, so instead, we run, numb and pretend, pretend like we're going to live forever.

When my momma was diagnosed with cancer, all the oxygen was sucked out of the world and ever since, well, ever since it's been a little harder to breathe.

We drove silently, she and I, to the doctor appointments where the news went from shocking to terminal.

I can still remember sitting in the front of that mirror, next to her, as big clumps of hair and little ones fell out too, fell out before she began pulling them out. I told myself to stay strong as she slipped beyond consciousness. But inside, I was a two-year-old throwing a fit, pounding my fist, and kicking my feet.

Death, death is unfair, especially when it takes our babies, the young, and our mommas.

WHAT IF death inspired us to live more audaciously?

WHAT IF we refused to let any good deed go undone?

WHAT IF we treated every encounter as if it was our last chance to love?

What IF, Dear?

Dear Rockstar,

When you were little, and we were baking cookies
after you downed three, you begged for another.

And even though I hated to see those fat little cheeks quiver,
I said no.
I had to.
And well that, my Dear, is the truth about NO.
No, isn't easy.

Declining invitations, opportunities, and relationships takes courage.
Who hasn't suffered from the fear of missing out?

Instead of rushing to YES,
imagine a gap arising between every situation you face and your response.

Evaluate your options, listen to your gut, consider what you value.
Choice by choice, decision by decision, life is made, Dear.

Refuse to allow maybe, kinda, and perhaps to dilute your life.
The best choices are those you make with a Resounding and Exuberant YES!

Own your No.

Elevate No to Superhero status.

Because No, No makes room for YES, Dear.

DEAR ROCKSTAR,

You were sitting on the end of your bed.
Your face was red and your eyes swollen, you'd been played, played for a fool.
You thought it was love, and then BAM, she was sucking the face of your
best friend.

"*Forget everyone; everyone lies.*" You cried as your splotchy sad
face, reddened.
You were done, done being duped.

I've been there. I remember the feeling of betrayal piercing my heart at
the dawning of my duping. How each fact, each illumination sent another
arrow deeper.

BETRAYAL KILLS; IT KILLS TRUST.

After I was betrayed, mostly I wanted to hurt someone,
to run away,
to get very, very drunk
and stay under the covers until next May.

Instead, at the intersection of heartbreak and betrayal, it dawned on me...
I could continue to play along, or I could stop and face my truth.
I didn't want to continue.

Good things sour. Great things go awry.
And when they do, sometimes the hardest person to be honest with...
is yourself, Dear.

HUMAN
~~DOING~~
being

Dear Rockstar,

I may have made you feel, once, twice, or even a hundred times as if you were a side dish, an appetizer in my life.

I still remember your bright eyes staring at me from across the dinner table, hopeful. Hoping I'd linger, linger longer, and maybe take you out for ice cream if you were lucky. And then how disappointed you were when I rushed off to that meeting.

How many times did you silently suffer, wishing I'd choose you only to watch me choose work, my next workout, or others?

I use to believe if I slowed down, I might be found out. So I rushed to do more and hurried to do it faster.

Dear, the world wears busy as if it were a badge of honor. It is not.

The true test of your humanity isn't what you do, it is your ability to be, just be.

And when you're able to be, Dear, you're able to show up for the people who matter most. You're able to be a part of all you are connected to. And, you'll never miss an opportunity to eat ice cream with those you love...

Be, Dear, just be.

me again

pay attention

something's not right

Don't loose your cool. Slow down and figure it out. Something has to change

Messages   OK

DEAR ROCKSTAR,

When I was a kid, whenever anger showed up, tears, welts, grounding, and shame were never far behind. It was like living inside an active volcano; you never knew when things would erupt.

The day I accidentally blurted out, "*Shut up.*" to one of my parents was an eruption day. That day the volcano left welts across my butt, the back of my legs, and my right arm slightly dislocated. I still remember my shame a few days later as I changed into my basketball uniform in the bathroom instead of the locker room for fear someone would see my battered backside.

It didn't take long for me to learn that anger meant pain.

It wasn't until I was face to face with my children's anger that I realized I was still scared of anger. There was a reason to be fearful when I was a kid, but as a parent, I needed to listen, not run away or try to make light of other people's anger.

Dear, anger is not good or bad; it just is.

When anger shows up, listen.
Never assume anger has anything to do with the situation at hand.
Be curious, commit to getting to the root cause and not just the triggers.
And when it comes to others' anger, make it clear, under no circumstances will you allow anger to erupt into physical, emotional, or spiritual harm.
Set healthy boundaries.

Anger, anger is a messenger, Dear.

LEAK
LOVE

DEAR ROCKSTAR,

There's trauma and then there's TRAUMA.
And for us, TRAUMA crashed into our lives as half of our adopted family
watched as a plane with the other half fell from the sky.

Before that, I had no idea a 6th grader, 3rd grader, and their mother, a
woman in her late 30's could end up with PTSD. How was I to know, you
didn't have to go to war to end up feeling as if you had?

I wish your teachers, counselors, and our family had understood post-
traumatic stress syndrome looks an awful lot like anger, rebellion,
depression, and a lack of motivation.

When you rush to judge others, when you label people as this or that, you
overlook the truth about most of us, Dear.

You see, most of us are in a fierce battle, a battle
to hang on to hope and overcome our TRAUMAS.

Most of us are walking around wounded, faking normal.

So leak love, leak love, everywhere you go, Dear.

Dear Rockstar,

I may have told you just once too often to fight for what you wanted and not urged you nearly enough to practice the fine art of surrender.

And this, of course, is because for most of my life, I wanted to be in control.

I treated life as if it were a tug of war I needed to win. I was as flexible as concrete and notorious for being in everyone else's business.

The ego will deceive you, Dear.
It will tell you, you are responsible for EVERYTHING and EVERYONE.
And it will convince you that if you adopt the path of surrender,
you'll suddenly win, most likely to fail.

Lies. Lies.
Letting go is not defeat.
Surrendering doesn't mean you don't care.
It means you understand control is not the goal...

Are your knuckles white?
Peace will find you when you turn your palms up
and surrender to the WILL that is higher than you, Dear.

Gratitude Junkie

DEAR ROCKSTAR,

The day eight digits went missing from my bank account, I didn't feel grateful, no, not one bit. More pissed off, blindsided, and yes, mad, mad as h-e-double toothpicks.

Make no mistake, Dear, I'm no saint, more proven sinner. At that moment, a million thoughts swirled, none, not one capable of earning me sainthood.

And then a question, a question so absurd it got my attention.
"What are you thankful for?"

As if, well, as if I had a million things to choose from!

"Thankful for?" I spit.

"No, really, what are you grateful for right now?"

Feeling as if I was being tested, in the way the American Broadcast Association used to run tests in the middle of my favorite radio song, I answered.

I am thankful I haven't killed anyone...
I am thankful my lungs haven't given out and that my heart is still beating, and that my kids are fast asleep.

And then the bird that liked to flutter outside the kitchen window began chirping, and of course, I was thankful for the fact that even when it feels like the sky is falling, birds show up and prove you wrong—I swear. They do, Dear.

Truth be told, on plenty of days not nearly as dark as this one,
I have struggled to acknowledge my blessings.

If I could ask for one miracle for you each day, no matter your circumstances, I'd ask for you to be overcome with gratitude upon waking each and every morning. And for this ritual to be so consistent, you'd transform into a gratitude junkie, yes, a gratitude junkie... Dear.

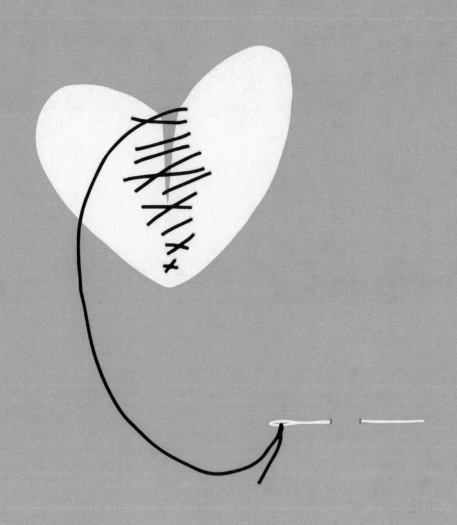

DEAR ROCKSTAR,

I used to play Judge Judy, pretending to be a goddess, doling out
forgiveness scantily,
blessing some and cursing most.

I convinced myself that if I were to forgive others, I'd be making their wrongs
right, even agreeing with their treatment of me.

In a short time, I transformed from stingy forgiver into transgressor,
the guilty "other" the offender, the woman who needed forgiveness
as much as she needed her next breath.

I slapped one of you, my dear Rockstar children.

I slapped you, once, twice, and three times across your sixteen-year-old-
cherub-like face.
I did. And for 523 days after, I waited, I waited for what I didn't deserve.

I waited for your forgiveness.

On day 523, you opened the door of my prison cell and released me from
what I couldn't free myself from.
You set me free from guilt and judgment. You did.

And now look at what forgiveness has done.
See how our hearts have grown intertwined?
Forgiveness frees. It frees you, and it frees others.

Forgive, radically and fast, and then repeat, Dear.

DEAR ROCKSTAR,

Do you.
Do whatever it takes.
Don't look back.
Do you, Boo, Boo.

"*It's a dog eat, dog eat world,*" the world shouts.

Love disagrees, "NO, DO US, DO US BOO, BOO."

I've been tempted to stockpile, hold back, and go it alone.
Life never worked when I did, Dear.

You aren't an island; no one is.
You belong with us, in community.
We are meant for each other, you and I, we are us.

**Community is;
an action,
a way of being,
a way of serving,
a way of loving,
contributing,
showing up,
speaking up,
and having each other's backs.**

So when the world says to look out for number one, remember you are part
of the whole, and we need you, Dear.

"I don't know what
I don't know. . ."

-Wisdom

DEAR ROCKSTAR,

Since the very first day of kindergarten, I was misled.
And maybe you were too.
Yep. Duped. We were.

I doubt it was intentional, but then again, maybe it was.
Every assignment I completed was graded based on the right answers.
Assignment after assignment, class after class, year after year
I was conditioned to believe learning was a destination.

Instead of answers, why weren't we taught to ask questions?
Instead of grades, why didn't we explore, create, build, and problem solve?
Instead of memorizing, why didn't we think critically?

Forget what you've been told.
Education is not learning.
Forget the answers; embrace the questions.
Forget the grades; follow your curiosity.

Learning isn't a destination rather a journey
fueled by the simple truth, *you don't know what you don't know,* Dear.

Dear Rockstar,

I'm quite sure you weren't born to be a laborer in everyone's dreams but your own.

No, you were born a CEO. CEO of your life.

And as CEO, your primary business is the business of designing a life, a life that fits you, a life you love. A life where you choose to spend your time and talents on what matters most and refuse to invest yourself in what doesn't.

CEOs of companies are responsible for the ROI, Return On Investment. As CEO of your life, you're responsible for your life's return on investment. (LROI)

A company may invest in cryptocurrency to harness access to the masses based on its vision, values, and mission. And you, well, what will drive your decisions?

What is important to you?
What will you give your time to, how much, and why?
What will you spend your resources on?
What talents, abilities will you develop?
What will you choose NOT to do or be or become?

CEO, CEO of your life. You are, Dear.

GIVE
GIVE
GIVE
ASK

Dear Rockstar,

What if everything you've ever needed is right here and always has been?

What if scarcity, the kind that causes heart palpitations when your account is overdrawn, when love ends, or dreams go up in smoke, is just our old friend... fear?

When I was an unemployed, single mom, launching a business with no resources, Scarcity argued I was too broke, too broke even to try.

Scarcity pulled up my bank account, pointed out my lack of assets, and illuminated my history of losses. And then *Scarcity* insisted I begin hoarding to remain solvent.

Instead, I volunteered to run with other people's children, and it helped erase my losses. I went back to school to get my Masters and discovered community. And I sat in coffee shops from morning to night with struggling entrepreneurs who, as I helped, illuminated the path for my business to succeed, they did.

And along the way, I learned, Dear. I learned the only way to suck the marrow from life is to give and then give some more. I also learned to open myself up and ask for what I needed, to receive the blessings others were born to share.

Give. Give. Give. Ask, Dear.

WHAT'S YOUR

DEAR ROCKSTAR,

As far back as I can remember, someone was telling me what to do,
where to go
and who to be,
until they weren't anymore.

Suddenly I was responsible for the answer to the question:
"What matters and Why?"

This question might just be the most critical question you'll ever ask, Dear.
The answer confirms your direction.

When the fog rolls in and all paths blur, take a moment to consider the end
in mind. Why are you on the planet and what, what matters?

And if you can't find your answer, imagine your life is over.
And before you're granted spirit hood, you have an opportunity to review
the highlights of your life, the best moments. Now see your life, from this
moment to your very last breath, scrolling on the screen in front of you.

What happened?
What was most important?
What mattered?
What was meaningful?

The quality of your questions determines the quality of your life.

"Why" matters, Dear.

DEAR ROCKSTAR,

How many Thanksgiving's did I spend locked in the bathroom at my
sister's house? Life wasn't what I'd ordered, not what I expected.
I dreamed of the fairy tale, you know the one, the one where Prince
Charming sweeps you off your feet. And the two of you build a castle, a
castle in the sky?

Well, there was a Castle and a Prince.
And then, before I knew it, I was Old Mother Hubbard with bare
cupboards.

I didn't expect my children to be raised in different houses by people,
people who'd been neither sperm nor egg.

I didn't expect there to be fissures, where once there was love.
Life rarely goes to plan; people and relationships are full of surprises,
Dear.

Some fissures are minor; others aren't. Some heal quickly. Others fracture
decades of trust and leave a hole inside of you so big you can't ever find
your way back to one another.

No one can tell you what is repairable and what isn't.
But, I will tell you that no relationship is beyond healing if two people
commit with all their hearts, minds, and wills to make it so.

And still, in this life of yours, you will have to choose which fissures and
fractures to tend to and which to break free from, Dear.

Radically Inclusive

DEAR ROCKSTAR,

Because, well, because I tend to be more Judge Judy than Mother Teresa, I often chant,
"*Wear their shoes. Wear their shoes. Wear their shoes.*"
This mantra triggers me to remember the other, the stranger, and the person before judging, labeling, or ostracizing them.

I know, I know. I've seen the research.
Understanding is not easy.
Humans are much more likely to be empathetic to people, people who look like us, whose skin is the same color. And furthermore, we're far more likely to be compassionate to people who vote like us.

So dear, prayers, chants, meditations, and intentions are a good start, but they are not enough. To drive out indifference, hate, and intolerance, we need to befriend people who don't look or believe like us. We need to build diverse communities.

Can you imagine what might be possible if we decided everyone belonged?

Imagine a world where strangers are welcome.
Where labels are replaced with questions.
Where judgment dissolves into grace.
Where understanding erases intolerance.
Where love displaces indifference.

Be radically inclusive, Dear.

TRANSFORM

UPLIFT

INSPIRE

create

unite TEACH

encourage

Restore

DEAR ROCKSTAR,

Do you remember when you were little, and I use to tell you stories of The Blackberry Fort? And how at the end of each story you would always ask me the same question?
"Is that true?"

I, well, I wanted to tell stories that stretched you beyond what you knew.
I wanted to use words to illuminate a perspective you hadn't yet reached.
I wanted to equip you to go back to the playground to confront the bully.

> *We gutted the middle of the blackberry vine, leaving a cave of winding rooms with halls leading to different size rooms. The ceiling was a thorny tangle, the floor a medium northwest brown with random rocks and blackberries, of course. Plastic lawn furniture and grey boat tarps covered our mismatched furnishings. We ate meals and read, used sleeping bags as rugs, and well, made it our fort we did.*

On your bed in the dark, I told you stories, each word I said painted a picture, a picture you created in your little head. Whether they were true or not, they helped you envision a new reality and sparked your imagination to create stories, stories of your own.

Words build.
Words destroy.
Words are power. Powerful

Choose them wisely, Dear.

DEAR ROCKSTAR,

I was impressed. You'd only been certified a week, and now you were serving your first client. I watched as you transitioned from consumer to creator, and my heart leaped; it did.

I want to warn you, Dear, consumerism would have you believe you are nothing more than a cog in the market. Culture would have you think your highest aim is to have, possess and consume. And if you give yourself over to consumption, you run the risk of becoming a slave to things and work that keeps you small.

Thankfully what makes life worth living is far more nuanced and beautiful than anything you could ever buy. You see, you know it, you do. You sense a purpose far greater than you imagined. You know you are here, here on this planet, to make a difference. And you know there are things only you can create and co-create.

CREATE, CREATE AS IF IT WERE YOUR BIRTHRIGHT, DEAR.

DEAR ROCKSTAR,

There's joy and there's happiness.

Are you rolling your eyes at me, wondering if now I've gone a page too far?
For no one, no one screws with happiness.
I admit, happiness gets a lot more press than Joy, yet still, if I had to pick, I'd
pick Joy.

And my reason is simple,
Joy is BOTH AND.

Joy stayed with me when happiness evaporated, she comforted me when you,
my firstborn, arrived just six grieving months after my momma passed.

Joy, she never left when my momma got sick, not even the rainy night after
we buried her, and I dreamed she was getting wet. Nor in the first few
moments of your life when we were together, you and I, without her.

Joy held space for exhilaration and grief.

Joy, Joy is a choice.
Choose Joy, Dear.

Love Juice

Dear Rockstar,

There's love, and then there are all its artificial replacements...
Approval seeking, ladder climbing, and people-pleasing are just a few of
its doppelgangers.

You know how obsessed I am with all things healthy, wheatgrass,
spirulina, and organic? Well, as much as I love health, there's
something I used to crave more.

The love juice.

I spent a good portion of my life chasing the juice, Dear.
You shake your head, wondering what I could possibly mean.

Love juice is nothing if it is not the "juice" extracted from others,
in the form of approval, recognition, attention, and acknowledgment.
An artificial replacement for the real thing, Dear.

A gulp of the juice gets the *I'm important* endorphins rushing, but, similar
to all replacements (think margarine) leaves you wanting.

Dear, the world will tempt you to believe likes, beauty, awards, promotions,
views, money, and power are what are important.
And as appetizing as these appear, they aren't the real thing.
They are fakes, I swear...

If you have to chase it or earn it, it is not love... Dear.

DEAR ROCKSTAR,

When I was in Bali the first time, beauty struck me.
It struck me like a love-sick teenager she did.

In the bright colored sarongs and delicate lace tops,
the ceremonial dress of the women.
In the folded bamboo offering boxes strewn with
frangipani and incense in doorways.
In the toothy grins of little ones,
older men, and slathered across the faces of the families of four
huddled together on the back of a scooter.

Beauty.

I have no idea why it took a journey around the world to open the eyes
of my heart, but it did, Dear. Beauty spoke so tenderly in this distant
land. In laughter, she shattered ignorance. In the bathtub, I sensed
her effervescence. And well, she even made a showing in the plate of
vegetables, cooked by a host and served on the floor.

Beauty hides in everything, always hinting, hinting of her source.
Reflecting, if you will, the awe, wonder, and mystery of the Divine.

I returned to the states with my palate forever changed.
I sensed it when I pulled the warm sheets out of the dryer.
When I stood under the tree and stared at the dirt as if, well as if I'd
never really looked at dirt before. And I felt it, really sensed it in smiles
not meant for me and in the way objects, even glasses sat so royally on
the bridges of other people's noses.

Beauty, may it open the eyes of your heart, Dear.

Whatever you have the **courage** to face, you can **overcome.**

Dear Rockstar,

I was born with enough energy to power a couple of hundred solar farms.
And so I ran, I ran a lot.
Anxious and nervous, I liked myself better when exhausted.
It seemed everyone else did too.

Movement and physical activity became saviors of sorts.
I used running the way friends used beer and vodka. The more life hurt, the
more I ran. The deeper the pain, the faster I went.

And because we become what we repeatedly do, I became really, really good
at running, and well, really, really bad at facing life's challenges.

Then my knees started shaking and a doctor told me I'd run through my last
bit of cartilage if I didn't stop. Now, I'm not about to lie and tell you it was
easy to stop running. No, it was downright terrifying.

But as I moved slower, as I refused to run every time life got tough,
I learned, I learned. I did.

You can change anything you have the courage to face, Dear.

Rx

COURAGEOUS
CONVERSATIONS

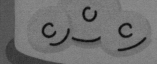
~~Dr Rockstar~~

Take whenever denial tempts you or
threatens you and your relationships.

Dear Rockstar,

Denial.
He is a coward, this dude.
Blatantly refuses to acknowledge reality; he does.
He's an expert at masking difficulties with that artificial bliss of his.
And to boot, a liar.

He's whispered a hundred times if he's whispered once to me,
"It will take care of itself, don't worry, just ignore it.
It will blow over. Don't bring it up.
Just give it time. Everything will be alright..."
Denial kills.

I know. He's killed a hundred relationships I know of, and well... everyday
I watch him try to kill more. If you aren't careful Dear, Denial will convince
you there's nothing to worry about when in reality, there is.

Refuse to ignore, refuse to turn a blind eye to what threatens your
life, relationships, and those you care about.

Trust you and God are more than enough for the most difficult conversation.
And then commit, commit to acting quickly, so Denial doesn't kill
what's most important to you, Dear.

eliminate the
TOXIC
MARINATE in the
POSITIVE

DEAR ROCKSTAR,

Fast. Cleanse. Organic. Gluten-Free. Vegan.
I used to be slightly, I mean entirely, OBSESSED with health.
In a fit to save myself, I swore off meat and embraced vegetables.
And when that wasn't restrictive enough, I swore allegiance to
Veganism.

One day during my yoga practice, my mind went from calm to a storm.
I was fuming. Why couldn't I focus?

Before I knew it, I was drowning in negative thoughts.
It was then I discovered my diet wasn't all I should be worried about.

Dear, there is nothing wrong with eating clean and making healthy choices.
And still, there is more to health than just your body and your diet. Your
mind, your thoughts, and your spirit matter too.

And although you aren't responsible for what comes into your mind. You are
responsible for what you do with the thoughts which show up.

What will you focus on? Which thoughts will you nurture, which will
you ignore? Which thoughts will you feed and which will be sent packing
promptly?

Seek to eliminate the toxic and marinate in the positive... Dear.

DEAR ROCKSTAR,

I once told your story to another and well, it wasn't my story to tell.
I broke your confidence. And the trust between us.
What I didn't know then, that I do now, is that every action and every word matters.

You see there's an ongoing trust bank account growing between you and everyone you care about. Consciously or unconsciously, we fortify or weaken trust every day.

Unfortunately, we see the trust breaches of others more clearly than we see our own.

Trust is the foundation.
It's the glue holding us together.
It grows slowly over time.
And yet, can be destroyed in mere seconds.

You will make mistakes, Dear, we all do.

When you break trust, take immediate responsibility.
Mess up, fess up and then dress up.

Trust, without it... there are no relationships, Dear.

WHAT ARE YOU WAITING FOR?

DEAR ROCKSTAR,

You've heard the saying, "Don't worry, there's always tomorrow?"
If you discern this to be the whisper of TRUTH, then, by all means,
be patient. Reflect. Even relax, Dear.

However, if this is not a subtle urge to calm down and reset. But rather advice
from a mere mortal, or worse yet, the voice of fear or procrastination... think,
think again.

Tomorrow, tomorrow is not guaranteed.

There was not a tomorrow for my momma. And tomorrow didn't arrive for
our dear friends Bob, Chris, Becky, and Troy after their plane crashed.

I dare say we all intend for tomorrow to arrive, but someday, well, it won't...

Reflect when you must, rest when it is the most important thing to do
and all other times have a bias toward ACTION.

Live a life of MASSIVE IMPERFECT action, Dear.

Say it NOW.
Do it NOW.
Take the risk NOW.
Ask the question NOW.
Seize the opportunity NOW.
Follow your dreams NOW.
Make the call NOW.
Send the gift NOW.

What are you waiting for, Dear?
Take a leap and START.

DEAR ROCKSTAR,

I once cried every day for a year and a half. I did.
I cried in the bathtub each night while the water was running, so no one
would hear me. And then one day, I was standing between the red onions and
the sweet potatoes. And all I wanted to do... was hug the produce man.

The world is not comfortable with our tears, Dear.
And so mostly, you will be tempted to hold them in.
I'd recommend not. Tears dissolve grief and allow the loss to leave your soul
if only, Dear, you let them flow.

My advice is to cry, cry as much as you feel like, and stop when you,
when you are good and ready and not a moment sooner.

And then after you are all cried out,
determine to hug as many people as possible.
Yes. After you are done crying, start hugging.

Hugs. No one gets nearly enough.
Tears. Few of us let them flow freely enough.

A great life consists of both.
Tears and hugs.
Cry and embrace, Dear.

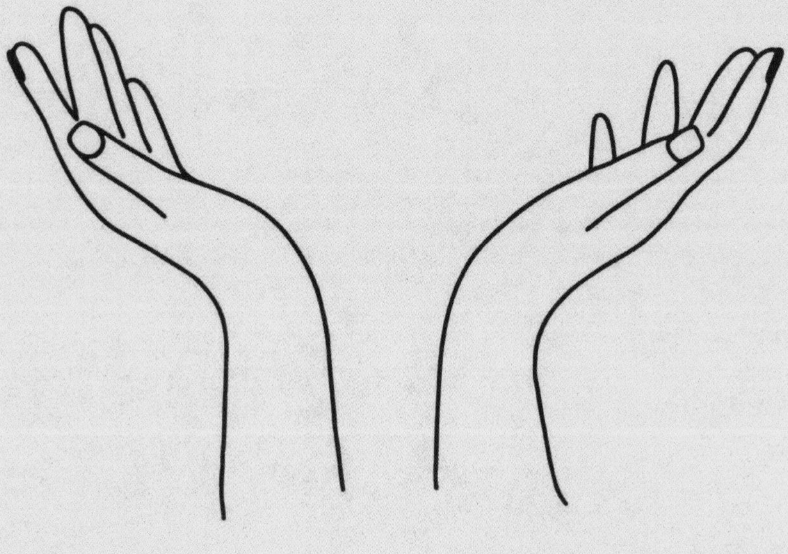

Dear Rockstar,

When I traveled in Thailand and Indonesia, I woke to find flowers in small woven baskets and incense burning on my doorstep each morning.

Offerings.

Every day the people made offerings to their gods.
As I watched their devotion, I mused, of course, it made sense.
When we devote time to creating beauty, we receive beauty.

And so I began considering how I might live if this were true.

How would I enter into each interaction?
What words would I speak?
How would I show up?
Whom would I be when no one was looking?
Who would I be to my employees, my team, my friends, family, or the homeless man on the corner?

Every moment is holy, all of life is an offering, your offering, Dear.

LIVE

STOKED

Dear Rockstar,

I can still hear the excitement in your voice. You passed the third round of interviews and were on your way to being offered the job. Stoked you were.

Afterward, you waited and waited and waited some more until finally you were told you'd been benched. As I watched your energy flow from excited to disappointed, I grew concerned.

I didn't want you to give up on your dreams. After all your hard work, I couldn't bear the thought of you going backward or resigning to whatever came your way.

Dear, the greatest travesty isn't that you fail. It is that you would give up reaching for the stars and instead settle for a life that didn't excite you.

Pursue a life that lights you up.

If it doesn't make your heart sing, if it doesn't challenge you and allow you to head in the direction of your dreams, it is not for you, Dear.

Stoked is your spiritual mandate.

Live stoked, Dear.

DEAR ROCKSTAR,

I remember a bout of laughter that still makes me giggle.
I was a reporter for the high school television station.
The cameras were rolling, 4,000 students watched as I began an interview
with the student body president.

"Good morning and welcome to Mariner T.V." I smiled into the camera. *"With
me today is our Student Body President."*

My guest explained that no one was purchasing prom tickets.
He paused long enough for me to ask a question, but before I got it out, he
blurted, *"If the Seniors don't get with it... the Prom will be canceled."*

I giggled. And one giggle turned into two, and before I knew it, the giggles
had baby giggles; they did. In an attempt to gain control, I opened my mouth,
and instead of a normal word, a soprano like screech rang through the studio,

"So, the Prom, the PROM is canceled?"

And then the giggles multiplied into quintuplets,
And the couch we shared shook as if we were in an earthquake; it did.
Finally, the teacher's face exploded with the command,

"Cut, cut, cut to a commercial."

Dear, life is funny.
You will get your undies in a wad, a time or two hundred, you will.
Don't take yourself so seriously.
Lighten up. Laugh.
Let your giggles have babies.
Because laughter, laughter gives life, Dear.

DEAR ROCKSTAR,

The most unstable thing I've ever thought is to consider ending my life
by parking my SUV on the tracks after my marriage ended.
I did consider it, Dear. But only for a few moments.

My mind believed I had failed and was not worthy of redemption.

A war raged within. My thoughts were crazy, and I, I was a hot mess.

Your life will be full of pivotal decisions. And if you are lucky enough to live
long enough you might just find yourself changing your mind and doing
things you never thought you'd do.

You are not the one who determines your worthiness, Dear.
Love is not something anything or anyone can disqualify you from.
No decision, mistake, or even sin can separate you from the unconditional
love of your Creator. Love has redeemed you, atoned for you, and is yours... if
only you accept it and refuse to allow fear to tell you otherwise.

You and love are one.
And peace, the peace that surpasses all understanding, is your birthright.

May you know the unconditional love you were born into, and may it
transform your life into a channel of peace, Dear.

"Where there is hatred, let me be love. Where there is injury,
your pardon Lord. And where there is doubt, true faith in you.
Make me a channel, a channel of your Source."

DEAR ROCKSTAR,

I grew up in a crazy-making house.
Not the straight-jacket, nut job kind, but rather the half-sweet, half-sour,
volcanic kind, the kind that's always bubbling beneath the surface.

Crazy-making is the condition in which hypocrisy runs rampant, in which life
and people lack consistency. In this condition, only one opinion matters, and
well, it's not yours.

Crazy-making is passed down through the ages.
It moves from one generation to the next, through the wounds of the child
inside parents who were once victims of crazy themselves.

Crazy making homes birth children who lack self-confidence,
children who are conditioned to gain the approval of others,
who are anxious, struggle to find their voice,
and cannot trust themselves and others.

It will take more than love to eradicate crazy-making in our lifetime, Dear.

It will take a commitment to create safe homes.
Homes where words are not used as weapons.
Where physical punishment is outlawed and abuse of any kind abolished.
And it will take recognition on the part of all hurting adults
to seek healing so they can love those they care about.

My hope is you will create a home where discussion and disagreement is
encouraged.
A place where all have the space to be imperfect, and respected.
A home where everyone is encouraged to nurture their opinions, voice and
becoming.
A place where no one is elevated above another.
A place where love reigns and where everyone is emotionally, physically, and
spiritually safe.

And then pray, pray, pray we all tread lightly and love more, Dear.

Dear Rockstar,

Being alone is not the same as being lonely.
And solitude despite its sister, solitary confinement, is not a
four-letter-word.

You don't need to be a yogi, pastor, or monk to benefit from
humongous swatches of time alone. Take it from me, the woman who refused
to get quiet until she was forced to...

I learned this when one of you, my Rockstar children, flunked out of school.
You were rebelling, or at least that's what it looked like then. Now I
understand you were just asking for help.

I feared losing you to drugs. So I sent you away to the Wilderness.
You hiked for 69 days as part of a 12-step program.

And because I knew you didn't flunk out alone, I committed to using the time
to do the work only I could do. I promised myself I'd find a way to heal what
was broken inside of me.

I scheduled three, three-day silent retreats to coincide exactly with your
three-day solo hikes. As you departed camp in Utah for an overnight hike
of 20 miles and three days of solo camping. I stole away across the Cascade
Mountains and locked myself in an old farmhouse.

With nothing to distract me, silence and solitude invited me to listen.
Feelings shrieked. Regrets named themselves. Scenarios rewound over and
over. Dots were connected. Confessions were made. Tears flowed. Prayers
were lifted.

Do whatever it takes to listen to your life speak, Dear.

EVERYONE WORSHIPS

SOMETHING

DEAR ROCKSTAR,

I remember a time you worshiped video games.
Yes, you. Try as I might, I could not pry you away.
Play, play it's all you did.

Something about the rewards, the safety, and the recognition you earned
completing levels and proving your competency made you obsessed.

I too, have lost myself, worshiped all sorts of things;
fitness, learning, building businesses, achieving goals
and a good twenty-eight other things or more.

What gets the best of you, Dear?

If you struggle to answer this, check your calendar.
Where do you invest yourself and your time?

Take a look at your bank account too,
where do your resources flow?

Everyone worships something, Dear.

DEAR ROCKSTAR,

I once was hired to let a team go
and when I did, snakes slithered out of the breakroom.

And there was a time, someone I loved
accused me of something, I never did, just because they wanted... something
I had.

Another time someone I knew told me... everyone hated me.

Dear. Don't get confused.

There are only two forces: LOVE or FEAR.

When the haters and naysayers show up shrouded in darkness, remember it's
really fear.

You can't win a war with fear. Don't try.
Furthermore, refuse to argue, negotiate, or even explain yourself to darkness.

Instead, feel the disappointment, grieve the experience, and
fill yourself up with love and light, when you are ready.
Muster all you have to send every bit of love, light, and blessings to those
haters and naysayers.

Light pierces darkness. Compassion heals.

Let no one's fear infection infect you, Dear.

We are creating a world where adults of every color, gender, size, & creed are restored to their role as creators empowered to finance their dreams and liberated to transform the world.

Dear Rockstar,

You and everyone you know and will ever meet were born for such a time as this.

Created to contribute, love and serve.

You and your friends are the makers, artists, designers, hackers, change-makers, social innovators, and entrepreneurs who will design lives of purpose, passion, contribution, and profit.

Do it in such a way as to secure freedom, equality, justice, and the pursuit of happiness for all.

Stay committed to the dream of ownership for all, of democratizing the ability for anyone to create value, their own income streams, or job.

Practice compressing time and de-risking your ideas before you take them to market to increase your success at creating economic engines and driving change, change the world, needs now.

Include everyone, leave no one behind, for when all are capable of providing for themselves, turning their ideas into reality and being the solutions the world needs now you will have strengthened democracy and improved mankind, you will, Dear.

WE ARE.
YOU ARE.

Makers, artists, designers, change-makers, social innovators and entrepreneurs committed to making the world better. WE ARE.

DEAR ROCKSTAR,

Why else would I be out of bed and back in bed so many times before finally relenting and beginning my yoga practice at 4 am?

It was the 25th of February. I'd been celebrating my momma's birthday without her for 26 years, but it never got easier. Inhaling, I brought my arms overhead. Exhaling, I placed my palms on the floor.

"*I'm proud of you.*"
Inhaling, I jumped backward.
"*I'm proud of you.*" The whisper whispered again.
Stinging, my eyes blurred teary.
"*I'm proud of you,*" This time, the words delivered chills.

"I did it," I responded as I lay down on my mat. "*I wrote the letters, I'm pretty sure you would have written if you had the time.*"

Rolling into the fetal position, I continued to talk with her,
"*When I'm there with you, and they are here, they'll have something to remind them of how incredible they are, how powerful they are when they join forces with the Divine. I can see them, I see them making lives they love, growing into forces, forces powered by love, igniting good wherever they go. They are going to rock, just like you rocked. Thank you, thank you for rocking my life.*"

All of life is your stage, Dear.
Your talents, experiences, and skills are your instruments.
Born to rock. Yes, you were.

Born to rock your one precious life,
like no one prior,
like no one after,
ever will.

TELL ME, WHAT IS IT YOU

PLAN TO DO WITH YOUR ONE,

WILD AND PRECIOUS LIFE?

Mary Oliver

EPILOGUE

The minute this project was stamped DONE. The next 10 letters
screamed to be written...
And as tempted as we were, at some point you must ship.
At some point you have to say, this is finished.
And so it was with Dear Rockstar.

What an amazing ride this multi-year, international, team based
collaboration has been. We are thankful for the editorial support of
Rosalie Wilmot and for Gwen Geivett's editorial contributions. And
thankful to all the readers who put up with reading draft after draft and
providing feedback on designs.

We hope our letters and designs inspire your spirit and awaken your
inner Rockstar.

IT IS YOUR TURN, IT IS YOUR TIME.

We can't wait to hear from you, make sure and find us
(#dearrockstarbook) on social and share your story -Dear Rockstar.

ABOUT THE AUTHOR

Pam Hoelzle is a mother, entrepreneur, educator and tech founder who lives in Seattle Washington. Pam received her Masters in Education at Seattle Pacific University and her undergraduate Marketing degree from the University of Illinois, Chicago.

Pam's contact information is pam@entrepreneur ready.com, and her phone number is (425) 218-5864.

ABOUT THE ILLUSTRATOR

Alicia Feinberg, although born in Louisiana, grew up in sunny Florida. She is a graduate of the University of Central Florida and received a BFA in Graphic Design with specialization in digital media. She specializes in hand-lettering and illustration in digital and print media.

You can find more of Alicia's work at aliciamariedesign.com.